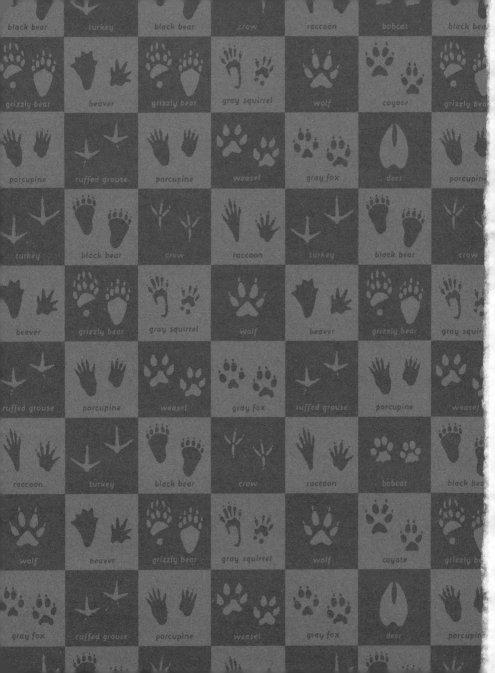

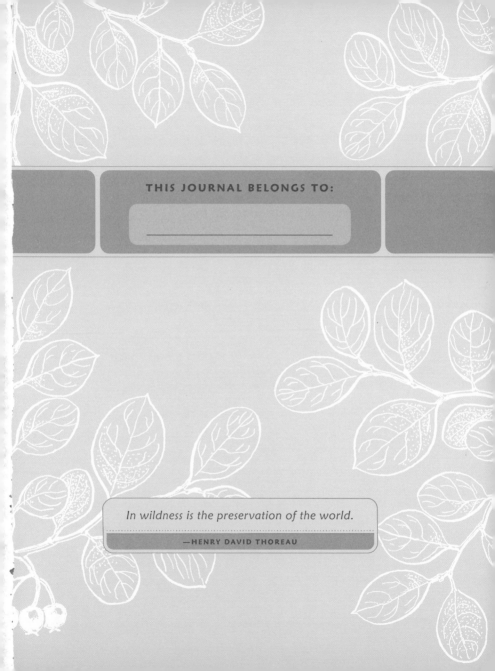

THIS JOURNAL BELONGS TO:

_____

In wildness is the preservation of the world.

—HENRY DAVID THOREAU

For more information about great nature walks and getaways, check out these sites:

- ♠ www.americanhiking.org
- ♠ www.audubon.org
- ♠ www.birding.com
- ♠ www.nps.gov
- ♠ www.publicgardens.org
- ♠ www.traillink.com
- ♠ www.trails.com

Potter Style

Cover Design by Jim Massey
Interior Design by Jim Massey and Jennifer Daddio
Cloud illustrations by Laura Palese

Animal tracks illustrations and information are courtesy
of the Massachusetts Division of Fisheries & Wildlife's
Pocket Guide to MA Animal Tracks. For more information,
please visit www.mass.gov/dfwele/dfw.

Printed in China

ISBN: 978-0-307-59091-6

Natural Notations

Some of our most reflective moments and rewarding adventures occur while walking in nature. The woods give us time to think, we start to notice the tiny details of flowers, we become more sensitive to the weather, we begin to listen more carefully. Don't let any of these moments pass you by—record your thoughts, observations, and nature notes in this journal, filled with helpful information for making the most of your outdoor explorations.

Use the reference illustrations in this journal to identify common tree leaves, plants, animal tracks, and cloud formations. Follow the prompts for ways to enhance your outdoor explorations. And don't forget to check out the destination ideas in the back of the journal. If you're wondering where to wander next, browse through the list of National Parks, noteworthy hiking trails, botanical gardens, and birding sites, so you'll never run out of places to explore!

Happy hiking!

TRAIL TIPS

Don't forget to bring (day hike list):

- water
- snacks
- map/field guide
- compass
- knife
- sunglasses
- sunscreen
- insect repellent
- lip balm (with SPF)
- matches
- whistle
- binoculars

- watch
- hat and/or bandana
- first-aid kit (Band-Aids, tape, Ace Bandages, Neosporin, moleskin, aspirin, Benadryl)
- extra socks
- sweatshirt/extra clothes
- raincoat/poncho
- tissues and/or toilet paper
- plastic bags or baggies for trash
- camera
- this journal and a pen or pencil

Even if you're just going for a quick hike, make sure to tell someone where you are going and when you expect to return.

Seasonal Suggestions

Each season boasts unique ways to experience nature in your area. Use the ideas below to help guide your observations and notations in this journal. Think about what else makes each season in your area special.

SPRING

- Notice when the various plants in your area bloom. Many plants have inconspicuous flowers that bloom before the leaves appear, so their pollen can be blown by the wind.
- Pay attention to which birds arrive early in the season and which arrive later. Observe which birds are just passing through on their way to other areas.
- Begin learning about edible wild plants—many will start to grow around this time.

SUMMER

- Take a walk on a beach and collect an array of shells, pebbles, and sea glass. Look for shorebirds foraging, fish jumping, or crabs scurrying, depending on the time of day.
- Try walking in the same area at different times of the day. Notice how the atmosphere of a place changes with different light and temperature.
- Go berry-picking or foraging for mushrooms. Establish some favorite spots.

AUTUMN

- Take a hike on a mountain trail to admire the foliage. Note which trees turn color first and which change later.
- Notice migrating birds and butterflies—they'll be either departing, arriving, or just passing through. If you pay attention, you'll begin to know when to expect them each year.
- Pick up some apple cider, a pumpkin pie, or some fresh fall vegetables from a farm stand on your way home. Plenty of delicious items are in season this time of year.

WINTER

- Learn to identify trees and shrubs by their bark, buds, general shape, and branching patterns. Find a tree identification guide that explains how.
- Find out which animals spend the winter in your area and how they spend the season. Some may hibernate and others might be quite active.
- Notice animal tracks in the snow and muddy areas.

Tree Leaf Identification

COMMON DECIDUOUS TREES

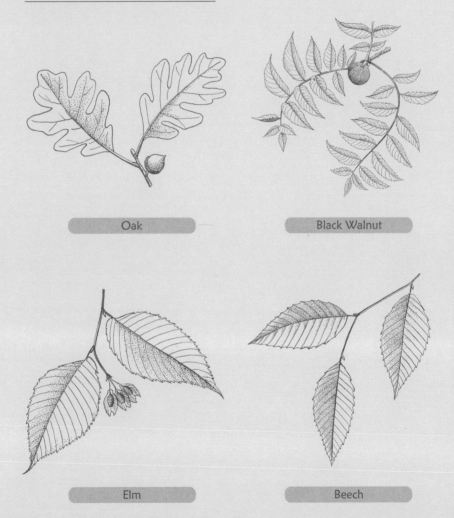

Oak

Black Walnut

Elm

Beech

Sycamore

Sugar Maple

Birch

Gingko

Tree Leaf Identification

COMMON CONIFEROUS TREES

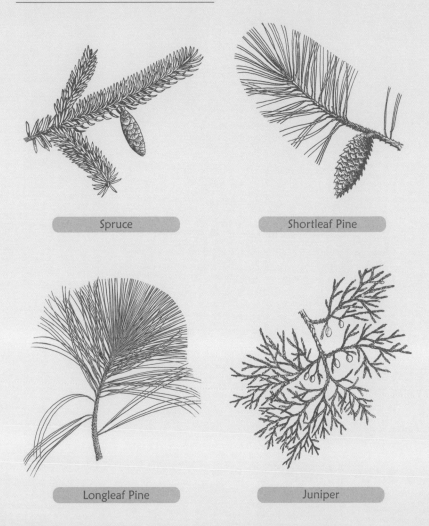

Spruce

Shortleaf Pine

Longleaf Pine

Juniper

Fir

Ponderosa Pine

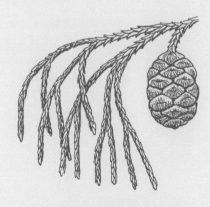

Sequoia

Redwood

Plant Identification

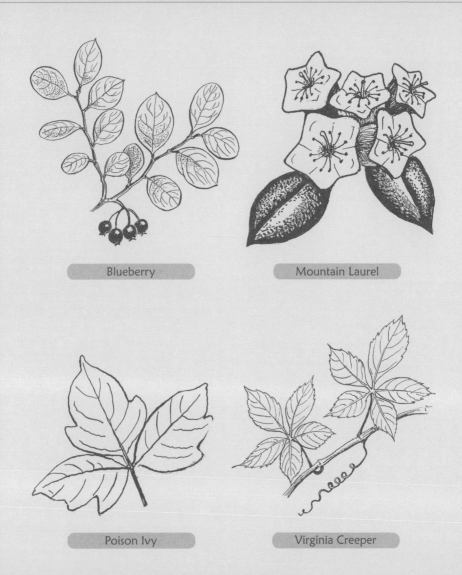

Blueberry

Mountain Laurel

Poison Ivy

Virginia Creeper

Identification: Trees and Plants Unique to My Area

Use this page to sketch and label any other trees or plants you find.

Animal Tracks Identification

Tracks will show considerable variation depending upon the condition of the ground (snow, mud, dust, sand, etc.) and the animal's movement. Please note: track illustrations are not to scale.

Key: H: Hind Track
      F: Front Track

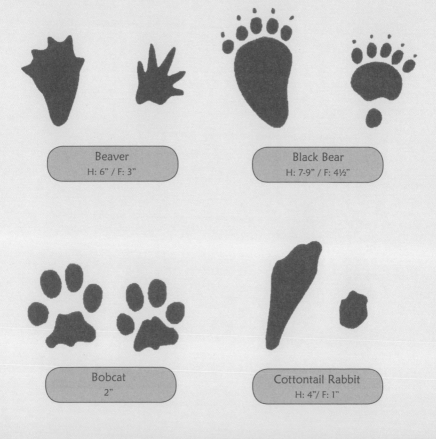

Beaver
H: 6" / F: 3"

Black Bear
H: 7-9" / F: 4½"

Bobcat
2"

Cottontail Rabbit
H: 4"/ F: 1"

Coyote
H: 2¼" / F: 2½"

Crow
2½"

Dog
2½"–4"

Fisher
2¼"

Gray Fox
H: 1¾" / F: 1½"

Gray Squirrel
H: 2¼" / F: 1½"

Grizzly Bear
H: 11" / F: 7"

Mink
1⅝"

Moose
4½"–5½"

Muskrat
H: 1½" / F: 1"

Opossum
H: 2" / F: 1¾"

Otter
3¼"

Porcupine
H: 3" / F: 2½"

Raccoon
H: 4" / F: 2½"

Red Fox
H: 2" / F: 2¼"

Ruffed Grouse
2"

Snowshoe Hare
H: 5" / F: 1½"

Striped Skunk
H: 2½" / F: 1½"

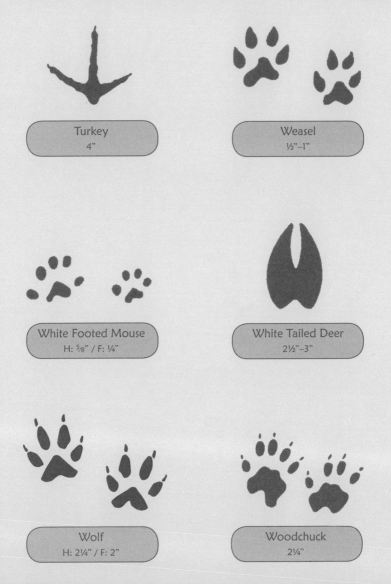

Turkey
4"

Weasel
½"–1"

White Footed Mouse
H: ⅝" / F: ¼"

White Tailed Deer
2½"–3"

Wolf
H: 2¼" / F: 2"

Woodchuck
2¼"

Animal tracks illustrations and information are courtesy of the Massachusetts Division of Fisheries & Wildlife's *Pocket Guide to MA Animal Tracks*. For more information, please visit www.mass.gov/dfwele/dfw.

Identification: Animal Tracks Unique to My Area

Use this page to sketch and label any other animal tracks you find.

Cloud Identification

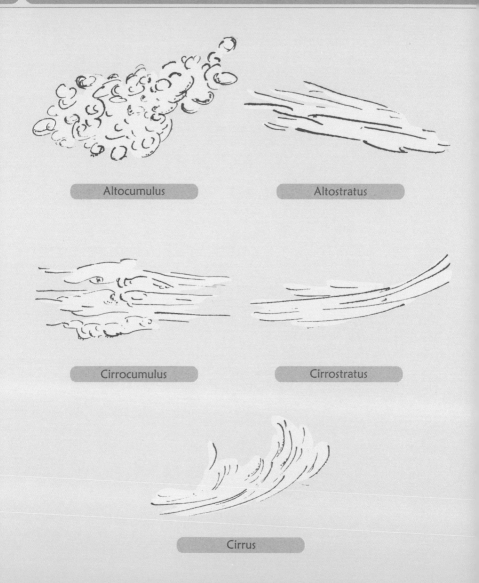

Altocumulus

Altostratus

Cirrocumulus

Cirrostratus

Cirrus

Cumulus

Cumulonimbus

Nimbostratus

Stratocumulus

Stratus

I like trees because they seem more resigned to the way they have to live than other things do.

—WILLA CATHER

The Lone Cypress

Pebble Beach, California. Dramatically shaped tree picturesquely perched on a rock overlooking the ocean; the trademark for the famous Pebble Beach golf course and resort.

Hunting and Gathering

What do you find yourself collecting along the trail? Colorful leaves? Wildflowers? Special stones? Mushrooms? Feathers? Make a list of things you like to gather.

I frequently tramped eight or ten miles
through the deepest snow to keep an
appointment with a beech-tree,
or a yellow birch, or an old acquain-
tance among the pines.

—HENRY DAVID THOREAU

The Angel Oak

Johns Island, South Carolina. Majestic oak tree with sprawling branches; estimated to be about 1,400 years old, stands 65 feet tall, measures 9 feet in diameter, and covers an area of 17,000 square feet with its crown.

Earthly Delights

Stop in your tracks. What do you hear? The wind, animal sounds, or bugs buzzing? What do you smell? Flowers, rain, or a nearby lake? What do you see? A colorful bird, mountains, or a strange flower? List your observations on this page and pay attention to all the little details.

The richness I achieve comes from
Nature, the source of my inspiration.

—CLAUDE MONET

The Luna Tree

(Also called the Stafford Giant) Stafford, California. Made famous by Julia Butterfly Hill, who lived on a 180-foot platform in the tree for 738 days to save it from being clear-cut; read about her experience in the book *The Legacy of Luna: The Story of a Tree, a Woman and the Struggle to Save the Redwoods.*

Petal Pages

Find a wildflower or two and press it within these pages. Which flowers did you find?

Why are there trees I never walk
under but large and melodious
thoughts descend upon me?

—WALT WHITMAN

The Senator Tree

Longwood, Florida. Largest Baldcypress tree
in the United States at 115 feet tall, with a trunk
diameter of over 17 feet; estimated to be
3,500 years old; named after Florida Senator
M.O. Overstreet, who donated it to the park
in 1927.

Picture Perfect

Paste in a postcard from a national park or trail you've visited. Describe your experience there on this page.

DATE:

WEATHER:

LOCATION:

Study nature, love nature, stay close to nature. It will never fail you.

—FRANK LLOYD WRIGHT

The Circus Trees

Santa Cruz, California. Over fifty-five imaginatively shaped trees were sculpted by farmer Axel Erlandson in the 1940s and 1950s into forms such as "Basket Tree," "Two-Leg Tree," and "Cube Tree"; most of the trees were transplanted and now appear at Gilroy Gardens in Gilroy, California.

Sky High

Look up into the sky. What kinds of clouds do you see? Do they resemble any animals, objects, or countries? Try sketching a few on these pages.

Between every two pines is a
doorway to a new world.

—JOHN MUIR

Chandelier Tree

Leggett, California. Impressive 315-foot-tall coast redwood with a six-by-nine-foot hole cut into its trunk for cars to drive through.

To me a lush carpet of pine needles or spongy grass is more welcome than the most luxurious Persian rug.

—HELEN KELLER

Natural Selections

List Your Favorite . . .

National park:

Trail:

Park or garden:

Birding location:

Body of water:

Season to experience the outdoors:

Kind of tree:

Kind of bird:

Kind of flower:

Snack for the trail:

Sketching Pages

Use these pages for mapping your trails, drawing observations, or pressing flowers and leaves.

* = UNESCO World Heritage Site

EAST

❑ **Acadia National Park,** Maine (islands on the coast; rocky cliffs; includes Cadillac Mountain, the highest point on the U.S. Atlantic coast at 1,530 feet)

SOUTH

❑ **Big Bend National Park,** Texas (800,000 acres of desert landscape; more birds, bats, and cacti than any other national park in the United States; one of the largest but least visited of the national parks)

❑ **Biscayne National Park,** Florida (colorful reefs, fish, and plant life; manatees and sea turtles; mangrove forests; remnants of pirates and shipwrecks)

❑ **Congaree National Park,** South Carolina (floodplain landscape; 2.4-mile boardwalk loop trail; canoe tours and backwoods hiking)

❑ **Dry Tortugas National Park,** Florida (seven islands composed of coral reefs and sand; famed for marine and bird populations; legends of sunken treasures)

❑ ***Everglades National Park,** Florida (largest subtropical wilderness in the United States; wetlands with mangroves, crocodiles, and many endangered species)

❑ ***Great Smoky Mountains National Park,** North Carolina and Tennessee (America's most visited national park; over 800 miles of trails; plentiful wildlife, including bears, deer, and elk; renowned for wildflower diversity, with 1,660 different kinds of flowering plants)

❑ **Hot Springs National Park,** Arkansas (nicknamed the "American Spa" for its thermal waters, cold-water springs, and bathhouses)

❑ ***Mammoth Cave National Park**, Kentucky (world's longest known cave system, with 365 miles already confirmed, dramatic chambers, and labyrinthine passages; approximately 1,500 species of flowers, as well as native grasses)

❑ **Shenandoah National Park,** Virginia (Blue Ridge Mountain range, breathtaking vistas; over 500 miles of trails, including 101 miles of the Appalachian Trail)

❑ **Arches National Park,** Utah (over 2,000 natural sandstone arches, unusual rock formations, dramatically colored and textured landscapes, plentiful crepuscular animals and songbirds)

❑ **Black Canyon of the Gunnison National Park,** Colorado (dramatic 14-mile-long Black Canyon along the Gunnison River, one of the steepest mountain descents in North America; animals such as mule, deer, elk, and coyotes)

❑ **Bryce Canyon National Park,** Utah (fantastic rock formations, canyons, and unique red rock spires called "hoodoos"; impressive night sky; mountain lions, falcons, and elk; arid landscape)

❑ **Canyonlands National Park,** Utah (strikingly carved landscape with mesas, canyons, buttes, deep river gorges, and scenic overlooks; desert bighorn sheep)

❑ **Capitol Reef National Park,** Utah (includes the Waterpocket Fold, a 100-mile-long fold in the earth's crust that is over 65 million years old)

❑ ***Carlsbad Caverns National Park,** New Mexico (desert and mountain landscape; prickly pear, cholla, sotol, and agave plants; over 110 limestone caves, including the Bat Cave, where up to 400,000 Brazilian free-tail bats take flight in search of insects each evening)

❑ **Channel Islands National Park,** California (encompasses five islands—Anacapa, Santa Cruz, Santa Rosa, San Miguel, and Santa Barbara; leaping dolphins and soaring bald eagles)

❑ **Crater Lake National Park,** Oregon (pure blue lake surrounded by cliffs and including two scenic islands; volcanic past; crest of the Cascade Mountain range)

❑ **Death Valley National Park,** California and Nevada (America's hottest and driest desert; sand dunes, multicolored rock layers, and canyons; 3 million acres of wilderness)

National Parks

- ❑ ***Grand Canyon National Park,** Arizona (one-mile-deep Grand Canyon; 5 million visitors a year; raised plateaus and scenic vistas; includes three of the four desert types in North America; the spectacular Skywalk spans the canyon)

- ❑ **Grand Teton National Park,** Wyoming (majestic mountains and glacial lakes; impressive wildlife, such as moose, bears, and bison; plentiful wildflowers, forests, and streams)

- ❑ **Great Basin National Park,** Nevada (includes 13,063-foot Wheeler Peak in the Snake Range; 5,000-year-old bristlecone pine trees; limestone Lehman Caves; cacti and wildflowers; exceptional stargazing)

- ❑ **Great Sand Dunes National Park,** Colorado (tallest dunes in North America; alpine tundra, forests, grasslands, and wetlands; creeks and streams)

- ❑ **Haleakalā National Park,** Hawaii (on the island of Maui; landscape ranges from arid to lush and verdant; coastal areas feature tropical vistas and freshwater falls; vividly colored plants)

- ❑ ***Hawaii Volcanoes National Park,** Hawaii (on the island of Hawaii; two of the world's most active volcanoes; bird refuge; carnivorous caterpillars; both desert and lush tropical rainforest landscapes)

- ❑ **Joshua Tree National Park,** California (plentiful Joshua trees and cacti; desert and mountain landscapes; striking canyons and rock formations; lizards and coyotes)

- ❑ **Lassen Volcanic National Park,** California (volcanic geology with steaming fumaroles and boiling mud pots; over 700 flowering plant species)

- ❑ ***Mesa Verde National Park,** Colorado (over 600 cliff dwellings of ancestral Pueblo people from A.D. 600 to A.D. 1300; first national park established "to preserve the works of man")

- ❑ **Mount Rainier National Park,** Washington (includes 14,140-foot Mount Rainier with glaciated peaks, 382 lakes, 470 rivers and streams; wildlife includes gray wolf, grizzly bear, and Canada lynx)

- **Petrified Forest National Park,** Arizona (brilliantly colored petrified wood; multi-hued badlands of the Painted Desert; historic structures and archeological sites with displays of fossils that are over 200 million years old)

- **Redwood National and State Park,** California (imposing redwoods, many of which are over 300 feet tall; grassland prairies; pristine coastlines, and streams)

- **Rocky Mountain National Park,** Colorado (extraordinary Rocky Mountains, with elevations reaching 14,259 feet at the weather-ravaged top of Longs Peak; stunning views)

- **Saguaro National Park,** Arizona (enormous cacti [saguaros]; mountainous landscape; wildlife includes coyote, Gambel's quail, and desert tortoise)

- **Sequoia and Kings Canyon National Park,** California (the world's largest trees; groves of giant sequoias; immense mountains, rugged foothills, and deep canyons)

- ***Yellowstone National Park,** Wyoming, Montana, and Idaho (America's first national park; Old Faithful geyser, hot springs, and canyons; plentiful wildlife, including bison, wolves, grizzly bears, and elk)

- ***Yosemite National Park,** California (one of the first wilderness parks in America; striking waterfalls, granite cliffs, deep valleys, and grand meadows; ancient giant sequoias)

- **Zion National Park,** Utah (deep canyons and towering cliffs of striking pink, orange, and red sandstone; arid climate; sparse vegetation)

NORTH/MIDWEST

- **Cuyahoga Valley National Park,** Ohio (follows the winding Cuyahoga—the "crooked river"; deep forests and rolling hills; wildlife such as deer, coyote, muskrat, mink, and raccoon)

- **Denali National Park and Preserve,** Alaska (glaciers, grizzlies, and caribou; sled dog demonstrations; North America's highest peak, the 20,320-foot Mount McKinley)

- **Gates of the Arctic National Park and Preserve,** Alaska (part of the Brooks Range, an alpine arctic mountain range; remote wilderness area above the Arctic Circle, far from any roads; bear country)

- ***Glacier Bay National Park and Preserve**, Alaska (tidewater glaciers, snow-capped mountain ranges, ocean coastlines, deep fjords, and freshwater rivers and lakes; humpback whales return in the summer to feed)

- **Glacier National Park,** Montana (pristine forests, alpine meadows, rugged mountains, and spectacular lakes; glacial-carved valleys in the Northern Rocky Mountains; over 700 miles of trails; more than 70 species of mammals, including grizzly bear, wolverine, gray wolf, and lynx)

- **Isle Royale National Park,** Michigan (island in Lake Superior, accessible only by boat or seaplane; highest backcountry overnight use per acre of any national park, but also one of the least visited; shipwrecks surround the rugged coast)

- **Katmai National Park and Preserve,** Alaska (volcanic landscape; famed Valley of Ten Thousand Smokes, a spectacular 40-square-mile, 100- to 700-foot-deep ash flow deposited by the Novarupta Volcano; remote wilderness; pristine waterways; rugged coastline)

- **Kenai Fjords National Park,** Alaska (shaped by glaciers, earthquakes, and ocean storms; includes the striking Harding Icefield—one of four left within the United States; wildlife such as bears, mountain goats, sea otters, and whales)

- **Kobuk Valley National Park,** Alaska (sand dunes 40 miles above the arctic circle; wildlife includes migrating caribou and grizzly bears)

- **Lake Clark National Park and Preserve,** Alaska (two active volcanoes, Iliamna and Redoubt; wildlife such as salmon, seals, and brown bears; impressive stargazing and the aurora borealis, which is best viewed in the winter)

- **Theodore Roosevelt National Park,** North Dakota (colorful badlands; prairie grasses and animals including bison, prairie dogs, pronghorn, elk, mule deer, and wild horses)

- **Voyageurs National Park,** Minnesota (shaped by glaciers; water-based park where you must leave your car behind to experience the lakes, islands, and shorelines; wildlife includes eagles, wolves, and deer)

- **Wind Cave National Park,** South Dakota (protects one of the world's longest and most complex caves; mixed-grass prairie and ponderosa pine forest; wildlife such as bison, elk, pronghorn, mule deer, coyotes, and prairie dogs)

- **Wrangell–St. Elias National Park and Preserve,** Alaska (largest national park in America at 13 million acres; includes the second highest peak in the United States—18,008-foot Mount St. Elias; historic mining sites; glaciers cover 35 percent of the park)

* = **National Scenic Trail:** *a designation for protected areas in the United States that are considered to be trails of particular natural beauty*

EAST

❑ ***Appalachian National Scenic Trail:** 2,175 miles (3,500 km), Maine, Vermont, New Hampshire, Massachusetts, Connecticut, New York, New Jersey, Pennsylvania, Maryland, West Virginia, Virginia, Tennessee, North Carolina, and Georgia

❑ **Benton MacKaye Trail:** 300 miles (480 km), Georgia, Tennessee, and North Carolina

❑ **Cohos Trail:** 162 miles (260 km), New Hampshire

❑ **Eastern Continental Trail:** 5,400 miles (8,700 km), Maine, Vermont, New Hampshire, Massachusetts, Connecticut, New York, New Jersey, Pennsylvania, Maryland, Virginia, Tennessee, North Carolina, Georgia, Alabama, and Florida

❑ **Finger Lakes Trail:** 563 miles (906 km), New York

❑ **Horse-Shoe Trail:** 140 miles (230 km), Pennsylvania

❑ **Laurel Highlands Hiking Trail:** 70 miles (110 km), Pennsylvania

❑ **Long Path:** 347 miles (559 km), New Jersey and New York

❑ **Long Trail:** 272 miles (438 km), Vermont

❑ **Mason Dixon Trail:** 190 miles (306 km), Pennsylvania and Delaware

❑ **Mattabesett Trail:** 57 miles (92 km), Connecticut

❑ **Metacomet-Monadnock Trail:** 114 miles (183 km), Connecticut, Massachusetts, and New Hampshire

❑ **Midstate Trail:** 92 miles (148 km), Massachusetts

❑ **Mid State Trail:** 327 miles (526 km), Pennsylvania and Maryland

❑ **Monadnock-Sunapee Greenway Trail:** 50 miles (80 km), New Hampshire

- **Northville-Placid Trail:** 125 miles (201 km), New York

- **Old Croton Trail:** 26 miles (42 km), New York

- ***Potomac Heritage National Scenic Trail:** 830 miles (1,336 km), Pennsylvania, Maryland, and Virginia

- **Robert Frost Trail:** 47 miles (76 km), Massachusetts

- **Sunapee-Ragged-Kearsarge Greenway Trail:** 75 miles (121 km), New Hampshire

- **Susquehannock Trail:** 85 miles (137 km), Pennsylvania

SOUTH

- **Allegheny Trail:** 330 miles (530 km), West Virginia and Virginia

- **Chief Ladiga Trail:** 33 miles (53 km), Alabama

- ***Florida National Scenic Trail:** 1,400 miles (2,300 km), Florida

- **Foothills Trail:** 76 miles (122 km), South Carolina, North Carolina, and Georgia

- **Katy Trail:** 225 miles (362 km), Missouri

- **Lone Star Hiking Trail:** 120 miles (190 km), Texas

- ***Natchez Trace National Scenic Trail:** 440 miles (710 km), Tennessee, Alabama, and Mississippi

- **Ouachita National Recreation Trail:** 223 miles (359 km), Oklahoma and Arkansas

- **Ozark Highlands Trail:** 180 miles (290 km), Arkansas

- **Ozark Trail:** 350 miles (563 km), Missouri

- **Pinhoti Trail**: 240 miles (390 km), Alabama and Georgia

- **Sheltowee Trace Trail:** 270 miles (430 km), Tennessee and Kentucky

- **Silver Comet Trail:** 62 miles (99 km), Georgia and Alabama

- **Tuscarora Trail:** 252 miles (406 km), Pennsylvania, Maryland, Virginia, and West Virginia

- **Virginia Creeper Trail:** 35 miles (56 km), Virginia

WEST

- ***Arizona National Scenic Trail:** 790 miles (1,270 km), Arizona

- **Bay Area Ridge Trail:** 500 miles (800 km), California

- **Bonneville Shoreline Trail:** 90 miles (140 km), Utah

- **Colorado Trail:** 483 miles (777 km), Colorado

- ***Continental Divide National Scenic Trail:** 3,100 miles (5,000 km), Montana, Idaho, Wyoming, Colorado, and New Mexico

- **Grand Enchantment Trail:** 730 miles (1,170 km), Arizona and New Mexico

- **Great Western Trail:** 4,455 miles (7,170 km), Arizona, Utah, Idaho, Wyoming, and Montana

- **Hayduke Trail:** 800 miles (1,300 km), Utah and Arizona

- **High Line Canal:** 58 miles (93 km), Colorado

- **High Sierra Trail:** 62 miles (99 km), California

- **Idaho Centennial Trail:** 900 miles (1,400 km), Idaho

- **John Muir Trail:** 211 miles (340 km), California

- **Oregon Coast Trail:** 362 miles (583 km), Oregon and California

- ***Pacific Crest National Scenic Trail:** 2,654 miles (4,271 km), California, Oregon, and Washington

- ❏ ***Pacific Northwest Trail:** 1,200 miles (1,900 km), Montana, Idaho, and Washington

- ❏ **Sierra High Route:** 195 miles (314 km), California

- ❏ **Skyline-to-the-Sea Trail:** 30 miles (47 km), California

- ❏ **Tahoe Rim Trail:** 165 miles (266 km), California and Nevada

- ❏ **Wonderland Trail:** 93 miles (150 km), Washington

NORTH/MIDWEST

- ❏ **Buckeye Trail:** 1,444 miles (2,324 km), Ohio

- ❏ **Chilkoot Trail:** 33 miles (53 km), Alaska and British Columbia (Canada)

- ❏ **George S. Mickelson Trail:** 109 miles (175 km), South Dakota

- ❏ ***Ice Age National Scenic Trail:** 1,200 miles (1,900 km), Wisconsin

- ❏ **Iditarod Trail:** 1,000 miles (1,609 km), Alaska

- ❏ **Knobstone Trail:** 58 miles (93 km), Indiana

- ❏ **Maah Daah Hey Trail:** 96 miles (154 km), North Dakota

- ❏ **Michigan Shore-to-Shore Trail:** 220 miles (350 km), Lake Michigan to Lake Huron

- ❏ ***North Country National Scenic Trail:** 4,600 miles (7,400 km), New York to North Dakota

- ❏ **Superior Hiking Trail:** 244 miles (393 km), North Shore of Lake Superior, Minnesota

EAST

- **Arnold Arboretum:** Massachusetts
- **Brooklyn Botanic Garden:** New York
- **Longwood Gardens:** Pennsylvania
- **New York Botanical Garden:** New York
- **United States Botanic Garden:** Washington, D.C.
- **United States National Arboretum:** Washington, D.C.

SOUTH

- **Dallas Arboretum:** Texas
- **Fairchild Tropical Botanic Garden:** Florida
- **Marie Selby Botanical Gardens:** Florida
- **Memphis Botanic Garden:** Tennessee

WEST

- **Davis Arboretum:** California
- **Denver Botanic Gardens:** Colorado
- **Desert Botanical Garden:** Arizona
- **Huntington Botanical Gardens:** California
- **Los Angeles County Arboretum and Botanic Garden:** California
- **The Lyon Arboretum:** Hawaii
- **National Tropical Botanical Garden:** Hawaii
- **Rancho Santa Ana Botanic Garden:** California

NORTH/MIDWEST

- ❑ **Chicago Botanic Garden:** Illinois

- ❑ **Dow Gardens:** Michigan

- ❑ **Missouri Botanical Garden:** Missouri

- ❑ **Olbrich Botanical Gardens:** Wisconsin

EAST

- ❑ **Audubon Center:** Maine
- ❑ **Central Park:** New York
- ❑ **Monhegan Island:** Maine
- ❑ **Seabrook Harbor:** New Hampshire

SOUTH

- ❑ **Black Mesa:** Oklahoma
- ❑ **Bolivar Flats:** Texas
- ❑ **Dauphin Island/Fort Morgan:** Alabama
- ❑ **Florida Keys:** Florida
- ❑ **Kiptopeke State Park:** Virginia
- ❑ **Okefenokee Swamp:** Georgia
- ❑ **Outer Banks:** North Carolina

WEST

- ❑ **Cave Creek:** Arizona
- ❑ **Elkhorn Slough/Moss Landing:** California
- ❑ **Madera Canyon:** Arizona
- ❑ **Morro Bay:** California
- ❑ **Ocean Shores:** Washington
- ❑ **Ramsey Canyon:** Arizona

❑ **Santa Barbara:** California

❑ **Upper Klamath National Wildlife Refuge:** Oregon

NORTH/MIDWEST

❑ **Attu Island:** Alaska

❑ **Cheyenne Bottoms/Quivira:** Kansas

❑ **Hawk Ridge Nature Reserve:** Minnesota

❑ **Lincoln Park Bird Sanctuary:** Illinois

❑ **Medicine Lake National Wildlife Refuge:** Montana

❑ **Muscatatuck National Wildlife Refuge:** Indiana

❑ **Pribilof Islands:** Alaska

❑ **Sault St. Marie:** Michigan

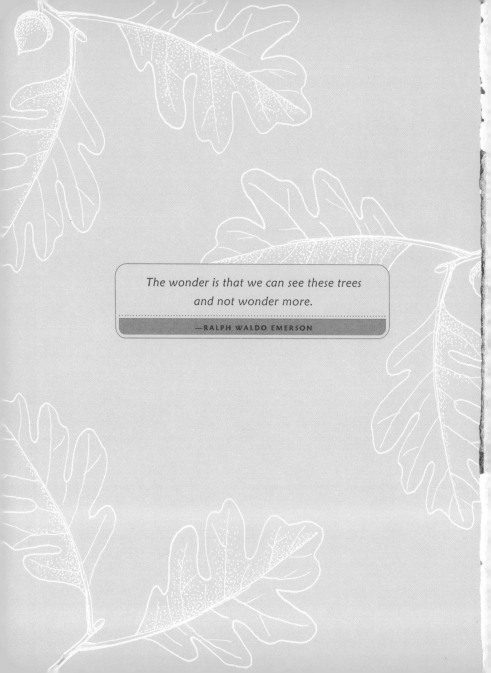

> *The wonder is that we can see these trees*
> *and not wonder more.*
>
> —RALPH WALDO EMERSON

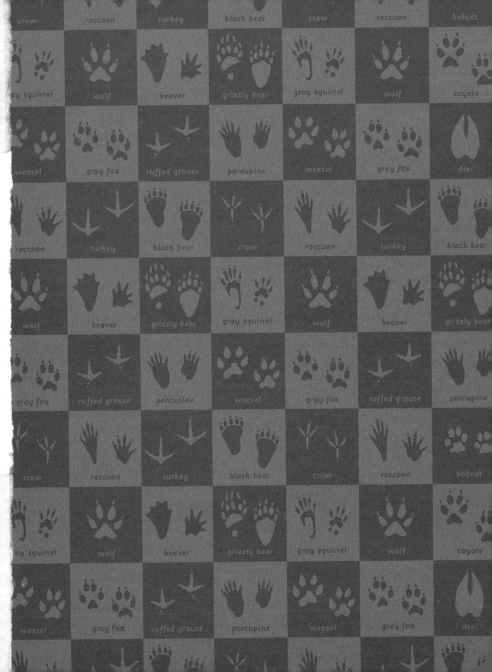